Anything but Normal

MAX ELLENDALE

Cover Designer: Ana Henriques
Editor: Deadra Krieger
Editor: M.A. Marino

Anything but Normal

Max Ellendale Publishing
www.maxellendale.com

ISBN: 9798838884978

For my whole heart, who is also my home. Without you, these words would've remained concealed in the darkness. With you, they lean into the light.

Amo-te, minha vida. Para sempre.

Anything but Normal is a collection of poetry and prose taken from my life experiences over the past decade. In all the years that I've walked this Earth, only one thing carried itself with me the entire way: words. In a full spectrum, from joy to sorrow, I'm happily horrified to share this work with you all.

To my faithful readers, thank you for supporting my work. I can't wait to toss more fiction at you from afar.

Cheers,
Max

Sol

We are both responsible
for the sun.

My unraveling comes
at the first crack
of your smile on every overcast morning.
Your gaze pierces the rain
and I see you
through the densest fog.
I'm called into being
by the very nature of your energy
and its pulse-beat cadence
as it swallows me whole.

We are both responsible for the sun,
but only you can make me see
through the rain.

THE RUINER

When I touch the world
it breaks.
I'm the ruiner,
the forgettable,
the denied.
Unnoticed
until again I reach for something
only to leave a pile of rubble in my wake.

When I touch the world,
it breaks.
I'm the path of destruction,
the cause for alarm.
Unseen and innocuous
until my poison meets your lips.
My nurture infects, leaves residue
on your skin, tainting
the angelic white with primal red.

When I touch the world,
it breaks.
I'm the last woman standing
at the twilight of a war meant only
for men, and sometimes for boys.

Avião

Words lock behind your lips,
tightening the contours of your neck.
I ache to rest my mouth
against the curves of you.
I wonder what you're thinking,
what you aren't saying
as your energy dims, pulling
you away from me.
We dance on the edge
between fear and meaning.
The heat abandons us,
leaving us stranded on a glacier pounded
into form by the strikes of beating hearts.
I look east while you west,
and I wonder if the ocean between us
has begun to show its storm.

Lua

We shared our first full moon in October.
A hunter's moon casting rainbows
through the clouds in a show
meant only for us.
I felt you most then,
with our twin gazes meeting in the middle,
and I understood that I loved you differently.
I'd spent all my life wishing
for you in the twilight.
My serendipitous girl, my third love
that I never expected and didn't deserve.
When your sweet greens dim in worry
that you're too much, and yet,
not enough, I'll remind you
each time luna casts her light on us together,
of the kiss we shared
under our second full moon.

I expect
to fuck it up.
I get so comfortable
in knowing that I've ruined it
that all I feel is relief.
Emptiness is home to me
and vacancy is a vacation.

Nothing speaks of aloneness
as much as a Saturday morning.
Waking up to the song of cicadas,
a cool breeze fluttering the curtains.
Warm and comfortable, wrapped
in soft linens. I should smile. I should
be grateful. And yet…
Sometimes I do, and I am, but mostly
I'm reminded
that I haven't heard my own voice in days.

NOVEMBER 3

You are the sun breaking an overcast,
peeking through the thick gray
to warm the cold.
I look up at you
and gaze at your light-born face
the same way I turn to the sky
in times of doubt.
I will always look up at you.
You're my constant
sky and sun
and my moon,
casting me in the twilight and dawn
of your affection.
You're my one reason
my one good reason
to stay.

I walk now, between the labyrinth
of bursting balloons and suffocating fish,
alone in a carnival set
for a woman of one.
Worthy of a glare, a seedy gaze, an entertained
guffaw.
Nothing more or less than
freak of center,
sodden under only the kindness
of the night sky.

When the clothes are off
and the moon is full,
I taste your sweet surrender.
Without a glance over
your bony shoulder, you exit
in the wake of a new dawn.
I only ever regret loving you,
ever drinking you, ever drowning
in the canopy of your hair.
And I remember
the way your last smile
never made it to your eyes.

Artista

I watch your hands when you draw.
That was the first thing I noticed about you.
Long, dainty fingers stroking colors on a page,
crafted from the way you see
the beauty in the world.
The languid, rich drawl of your voice,
when you say my name
and words like *beautiful* or *spaghetti*.
I see it all, and I rise. My feet leave the earth
and the ground falls backward.
I am elevated by you.

And then the universe reminds me
of my place
and reason becomes no match for pain.
We sleep differently, eat similarly,
but live with the ocean between us.

STUPID TWICE

I've done all of this before
the familiarity of it irks me.
Counting time, feeling trapped.
Why have I allowed this again?
The anchor becomes a burden
an added barrier to the distance
already suffering at the core of lonely hearts
marred by loss and fear.

At first wake, cracked open
in the light of *mourning*, I'm tortured
by the possibilities, made weak by
the fabric of time unwilling
to bend to my conjuring.

What have I done?

I touched the world again
and it broke.
Last time I was the collateral damage
but this time, it might be you and the thought
of your pain haunts me more
than my own ever could.
The most difficult thing in this world is to live in it
and perhaps a dead life bathes itself in the solace
of emptiness.

Gatinha

Your sweet voice, a vocal tremor above erotic,
soothes a longing that aches to be quenched.
It's so easy to rush, to push, to want.
I scream inside, for answers,
for clarity, for signs. For curses on
the distance and the predicament
that found us on the opposite side
of three-thousand miles and eight hours.
One whole sleep apart.

I watch you twirl your hair.
Pouty lips trying not to smile,
and flirty eyes flickering with shyness.
Your brow smooths in thought,
words unspoken, perhaps a match for mine.

My head longs to fall to a pillow beside yours,
and my hands ache to touch, to revel
in the warmth of your humanity
and the energy of your universe.
We share ghosts in the moonlight,
unravelling the tethers that ground us
from too fast, too far, too long.

Your smile in the morning,
the first image of my day,
breaks the surface of loneliness,
reminding me of what matters
and what waits.

Eu Vejo

The things she says to me
are the wishes I've made
to every night sky,
on every shooting star,
on every birthday cake.
I've wished for her longer
than she's been alive and now
I know why I've waited so long.

I awake to the world, bound
by a force that writhes
and seizes with anticipation
rocking and quelling only in the solace
of hers.

I can only hope
that on my next revolution around the sun,
I won't have to wish for her, and wish only
to keep her.
Every day, I will wish to keep her.
I've been sightless, but with love,
I see.

Areia

Fantasies break the morning light.
They wake me to flash through
my mind, in a tortuous shuffle.

Every scenario, terrible, incredible,
indelibly carved into my psyche
retracting only when movement begins.

Action is the enemy of thought, of emotion,
of slowing down the yearning that threatens
to destroy all I've ever been.

Part of me expects the ending.
Waiting for the day when too little
becomes too much and I push
so far and so hard that you fall away,
and I am left standing over the ruins
of something I loved.

Everything I've ever dared hold left me
in an ancient city carved from the rubble
of my loves and the sand dunes shed
by my dying heart.

BOX

Every time I believe I'm something,
I'm not.
I'm a swimmer
who can't swim.
A writer
who can't write.
A fighter
who can't fight.
I'm all and nothing at the same time
in a vessel understood only by Schrödinger
and his box of pussies.
Open me, reveal my quantum superposition.
I am both dead and alive until you look at me.
I am a thought experiment,
in love and in hate.
I am something and nothing.
I am a subatomic event
that may or may not occur.

BREAKER

My energy slams shut
at the slightest skid of rejection.
I close off, fold in, and push
away so hard that you feel it
across the universe.
The look on your face,
confusion tangled with hurt,
when you sense my withdrawal, and question
if it's you or something you did wrong.
It won't ever be you.
My ego suffers
when I touch the world and break it.
I am reminded of my venom.
I touched you, for one moment, and you broke.
A tiny, hairline fracture unseeable
on most days but lingers beneath until
the moment I touch it again.

Cansada

I wake up tired
on mornings without you.
It sticks with me like lead boots
bolting me to the Earth when
all I want to do is fly.
Nights with your warmth, your voice,
your rich languorous tones, coy whimpers,
and pleasure-filled breaths deliver
a wholeness to the vacancy
carved out of my soul.

The day wears on me, and your vibrance fades,
leaving in its wake the residue of you.
And when night falls again,
I look up to find the ever-present sky
and a crescent moon cutting like glass
the somber blue.
I am soothed only by knowing
we share the same moon.

Eyes open to the clear, cool morning.
Autumn burns the horizon, scoring
the skyline in brown-gray.

In the dying season, when flora
seeds the earth with its loss,
I am a bouquet of doubt in full bloom,
cut from the roots of all I've ever known.

I can't run or recoil or hide
away from the sun when the trees
lay bare against the sky.

I'm left
with the gravity of it.
A storm passed, only in silence
amidst the debris at my feet.
The calm outside doesn't reflect
the remnants churning still in me.

Space around me screams
with your residual essence,
the scent of your shampoo on my sheets,
the heat of your palm still burning
in the center of my chest.

TOO MUCH

Your energy quells to quiet
pulsations and I feel you
dim.
Words lock behind your lips
and your throat tightens
with every gulp.
The ones you don't speak
scream louder than the ones
that steal your voice.
Your gaze, flickering and downcast,
divulge your truth and I know
you're taken
by the heavy hand of doubt
brought on only by hoping
a little too hard.

What you don't say to me hits
harder than what you do.
I can see you, see to and
see through, knowing
someday those words
will tumble from your lips
to a heart that beats
only to hear your song.

THIRD LOVE

I've been living without breath,
A century or so it seemed
until the day I saw you smile.
Not just a smile or a guffaw,
but an embodied grin that made it
to your eyes. Sea-green and bright,
lighting the path for me and all I want
to do is follow. And create. And see.
But mostly, believe.
I never expected you. I never knew
that I could want something so much
and yet not lose myself
to the psychosis of yearning.

AFTER

When I lose myself, I risk you.
The numbness washing through me
like an ice storm
sweeping a rain forest, freezing it
at its roots. I did this. I did it,
because I am the storm and I
have met my end.
I loved
too quickly, too deeply, and the fear
of losing you lost you anyway.
I felt so much that I began
to feel nothing. I've done this.
I've done it.
Again.
I wanted different. I wanted
to feel, to die under the strength
of my emotions for you.
Maybe it's too late for me to unlearn
how to stop committing emotional suicide
every time I love something
as much as I loved you.

FALLEN

On the edge, so close.
Standing. Standing.
Holding on and standing.

Then a disruption, a pain of accident.
Tears come and break
my stance.
I fall and then I'm falling
not standing, falling.
And falling.

The sun is bright, reflecting
on the river in rippled circles.

    From heaven, opening and closing
    a target.

        And falling.

            And fallen. Fly.

ROT

For moments now and then,
I know what it's like to be a corpse.
Organs sucked dry and scream
for sustenance, for freedom.

Emotions run cold, numbed to
deepest depths like a
seabed of
the soul.

Charred remnants of anger
remain, the only hints of
humanity left in a sodden
heart.

Enflamed with wishes to tear,
thrash, destroy. There's nothing
like a death inside, of vessels frozen
encased in a chrysalis of torment.

A light from above,
wavering beacon.
Betrayed by sight. A lump in
the chest, awakened knock, a memory,
and faint flavor of hope.

AUSSIE

Curtains blow,
carried by the breath of

the sea.

Reminders of eucalyptus,
rugged and crisp.

Scented by the heat of day,
in the solitude of the
swooping magpie.

At times I imagine a world, a life, without alarm clocks. Where comings and goings are as natural as the flow of a river, or the advance of a storm. In this world, thinking and feeling are freedoms awarded at birth and fostered without constraint. Hierarchy doesn't exist in any form; man has no dominion over man or beast. And deviance or betrayal are handled with the even hand of natural order and survival. The first thought of daybreak is, "I'm awake," and not marred by the pressure of unfinished business. Where man is not in the image of God, but God is in the image of man. And animal. And plant. And soil. Breakfasting in strawberry fields and orchards. Or at the shore of sandy beaches as the morning sun breaks the horizon. There is no sound beyond the wind and waves, perhaps the distant cry of a predator mounting its prey.

UNTITLED

It hangs there at the tip
of a branch so precariously placed,
as though plucked with divine purpose and set
an inch from death where the wind bashes and
lashes, threatening to tear its hold.

Sometimes I wonder what the trees see, so high above
the rest of the world for centuries or until its trunk
meets the axe that turns it to paper.
Or what the leaves hear, swaying in the wind, jingling
with the aristocratic arrogance that they are indubitably
entitled, taunting those less pretty, less changing until
the celebration of their timely death in a sea
of red and orange.

I wonder what they think as they tumble, or float,
to the ground, one on top
of the next, mashed
under the winter snow then washed
away in the rain of spring.

Sometimes I wonder, when I stumble upon the veined
skeletons, brown and brittle, if it's proper to bury them
or let them decay.

I wonder if, maybe, the tree mourns its loss or if
the leaves know they have lost a sister.

NIGHTMOODS

Crickets sing with croaking frogs,
a breeze
like fingers of ghosts through my hair.

In the twilight of an August blue,
these are my nightmoods.

Hills tucked east of lake,
the pulsebeat
song of ancestral celebration.
Drumming, thrumming rapt joy
and sorrow tangle with the arrows
of Orion.

The hush
left soft and sweet
no less
than a lullaby.

WANDER

It is in my nature to travel,
northward in the fielded greens of unwielded
earthen control. To the valley of dreams
tucked away behind the wind-whipped barn,
yellow and flaking in places once smooth
and superior.

Where an oak lay fallen, roots exposed,
a cavern in its place,
my feet find solace in the soil that squishes
unwelcomingly, the only form of protest it has
ever known.

In the vale, where the crows cry
unseen from the heavens
and worms squiggle to safety,
my visions untame and lash,
voices unheard, too long to bear.
Back against the bulk of another,
I brace for assault
gulping for air
that never seems to satisfy,
never accustomed to the forces inside and out, writhing
in the sea of violence
driven only
by the pull and push of a storm.

KITTEN

I dream of the day you found me there
alone and waiting for someone
to lift me off of the tracks.
In a wave of crimson,
blurred emeralds, pure
and sweet, pull me
from the depths.
I am
yours.

LET GO

In the wake, drawn down by undertow
in emptiness and despair I
sink slowly, to the seabed
a place to rest my hair.
Beneath the sirens
calling me home
to crash, and
break over
me.

PAINTED

The day we met, masks removed for our
first kiss, we knew. Our halved souls met
their whole. People like us, like
displaced starseeds in
a galaxy
dressed
blue.

UNTITLED

In the rain sitting on
a white chair, water runs
down the legs held close
to you. Tears mingled, thinking
you can hide them from me
but you can't. Sadness and fear
radiates to a place of transcendence
and asks for holding.

Your hair, once crimson, darkened
and laden with the weight
of pain unhidden.
Come out of the rain, I say.
I can't, you tell me,
so I'm in the rain with you,
pattering and dripping from eyelashes.
Kneeling in front, you look at me
and smile. Smiling in the rain.
Thunder claps, your fingers
are cold. Get out of the rain, you tell me.
I'm not going alone, I say.
Your hand squeezes mine.
Two can come out of the rain.

PHANTASIA

Rushes of you,
cold and distant,
pictured against the backdrop of bathroom tiles
in an image not meant for me.
I'm shredded at the thought
of your body tainted
by the touch of another.
Big hands sculpting sharp hips,
supple breasts, then stabbing,
breaking you in,
and the destruction in knowing you enjoyed it.

Ghosts chase me down
whispering reminders in my ears
that keep me haunted,
keep me seeing and knowing.
I ache to replace that touch,
covet its erasure.
To soothe and cure you
with feathered caresses.
I crave the subtle art
of bearing witness to your pleasure,
and the succor that comes in knowing
that I caused it.

THIEF

Sometimes I look at you
and can't turn my eyes away.
I'm mesmerized by the glow of you,
the strands of your hair as they tumble
over sharp, curved shoulders,
how the morning sun sets your eyes to twinkling,
as you daydream at the trees tapping on the window.
I'm stolen by you,
out of this world and into the next,
a transcendence familiar to me only
in the context of you.
You move me,
like a ship rocking on the surface
of an ocean caught in wind-waves
and their swell.

NORMAL

I will never know normal.
To gaze upon someone
Without envisioning their death. The brutality
of it or the aftermath of
a suicide.
Rolling scenes of purple faces,
blood pooled and
the finding.

I will never know normal.
To look at a child without
worry for their victimization.
The hopeless powerlessness
that comes with knowing
their truth.

I will never know normal,
of a simple handshake
or a genuine smile.
Of a hug without meaning
or courtesy of a pause.

I will never know normal
because normal
has never
met me.

DECEMBER 28

She takes your breath away.
Do you know what that's like?
To have your own breath stolen
in a moment? I hope you do.
My god, I hope you do.

You fall asleep on her all the time
because you've never known safety
and with her, your body and mind
rest.
And you are resting
because you are home
and you are home together.

Then one night, you open your eyes
and wonder
how you ever lived without her.
How you managed to take a single step
without her hand in yours. And you know
she is your always.
Like every last line in a well-written romance novel,
she is always.
And she is all there ever was.

ANYTHING I'M NOT

I am not a poet.
There is nothing
lyrical or rhythmic

about me.

I am not a memoirist.
I am not nonfiction, nor
essay, or opinion.

I am fiction.

I am a wolf and a zombie,
A vampire and fairy. I am
sometimes a vixen caught

in a triangle of paranormal love and lust.

I am a child and an
adult. A murderer and victim.
I am a villain and

a hero.

I am fire and wind tangled
with desire, love, and revenge.
I am a witch calling the earth

to take on the night, and the rain
that washes it away in the morning.
But I am certainly not

a poet.

Today breathes like summer.
A pulsing promise casting temporal lines
in an impetuous ocean.
I used to think of myself as watercraft,
rolling along with the waves
of experience, of virtue.
A controlled buoyancy
quelled by the predictability of a liquid life.
Now, I am on the wind,
thrashed and grabbed
by every turn of a tornado.

Little death
washes over me
like a warm numb
quelling thoughts
and feelings in
a sarcophagus of nothingness.
An element of blank
disconnect from life
and humanity
looking right through but
never at.

Heavy fog settles
marring my experience
silencing my voice.
My mind tells me to
give in and up
to settle for less and
abandon what I loved
what I worked so hard for
what I deserve.

Little death
tastes delicious
syrupy sweet and
sexy enough to entice
a mind most chaste.
A lick into madness
of endless sleep
pain-laced movement
angry faces of dismissal.

Today I am a little dead
and little death
is my friend.

GHOSTS

"You look beautiful," I say, when I mean, "Why aren't you mine?" Fingertips graze the firm, satin lavender stitched only for her. "You feel different," I say, but I think, "I want this off you."

We smile together.

And always laugh.

"Your hair is so long," she says. "All I want to do is touch it." "You'll never be alone," she says. "I'll always take care of you. You're not alone anymore."

Then why am I? Why aren't we?

"You can move in with me. You know that," she says.
And I hear all the promises unkept.

Her hands in mine, cold and corpse,
warmed only by connection.
Ticklish nails, black-swept lashes, dimmed,
and shadowed,
flickering candlelight and fireworks
in our champagne.
Goodbye is three times,
see you later four.
That one last look
over her naked shoulder.
And we aren't,
because we couldn't
because we didn't know how.

Diamante

I wake before her
with purpose. To breathe
before she does.
To see her hair, perfectly night,
strewn across white linens.

Hands curled between her breasts
clasped fingers around her
dim-lit ring.
To watch her chest, fall and rise,
in time with the breathy wind pulsing
through the cracked window.

And when she finds me after
her own pursuit
her smile, curved cerise fruit
and for me, oh how she looks at me.
First touch of every day
draws me to life, to wonder,
to want.

My arms around her, still hot from sleep,
and a sigh meets my neck
when we know our homecoming.
Homecoming of morning
and the farewell of night.

"Dress for me?" I ask her. "Let's play."
She laughs, her smile brightens
cerulean blues.
"In heels?"
"Yes. And that black dress. You know the one."
"You just like watching me, " she says, and
I smile.
"I'll watch you forever."
"You'd better."

Her heart beats
in time with mine and
sometimes I can't tell if
she's inside me or out.

A laugh and I'm caught
in a tidal wave kiss,
then touch pours
drowns, devours…

She is mine and
I watch her,
in that dress
with smile-curved lips.

And I know she is
within and
without.

GOODBYE

Above the canyon, sandy stone in layers
flattened and coarse.
With red dust on my boots,
I think of you.

Wind tosses the shawl from my shoulders,
your voice in my ear as I lift it from
the ground.
Dusting it off,
I think of you.

My car by the side of the road, empty
and alone, on my knees in the mud, wisteria
in my nose. Tears wash the soot from
my cheeks.
With a flat tire,
I think of you.

The road is long and crooked. I stumble
but keep going. Where the moon hangs
low enough to kiss the earth and graze
the silos that reach for it. I break
like a lullaby,
mourning the night.
With nothing left,
I think of you.

And when I find myself miles away
perched upon a cool stone with lake breeze
on my skin, you hold me and
I think of you.

ABOUT THE AUTHOR

Max (she/her) grew up just outside of New York City, spending most of her formative years outdoors creating wild ghost hunts with neighborhood kids, setting booby-traps to capture unwitting family members, and building clubhouses on top of ten-foot walls. Max wrote her first story at the age of twelve and titled it Circles of Friendship. Through the years, Max has written several short-stories and poems, all of which met the wrath of the "Not Good Enough" monster and ended in fiery demise.

Max regained her confidence when she began writing scholarly articles and research theses on her first trip through graduate school. It took several years for her to break the habit of the formal writing that marred her creativity. Max writes primarily LGBTQ+ sci-fi/fantasy, crime/thriller, and romance stories. Max describes her women-loving-women novels as "edgy romance and crime/thrillers about women rising from the ashes of their experiences and thriving in the context of love and relationships."

TITLES BY MAX ELLENDALE

Four Point Trilogy
Four Point
Point Two
Mirror

Sapphic Romance
Skyclad
Midsummer
Try Pink & Indigo

Four Point Universe Romance Series
Anita
Wildrose
Rabbit
Mermaid
Hart & Stocker
Entanglement
Nocere
Moonflower
Relevé
Borrowed
Mercy
Solanum
Maverick
Jawbreaker
Infinitum

The Legacy Series
Glyph
Birthrite
Sacred
Bound
Marked
The Wolf's Consort

www.maxellendale.com

www.ingramcontent.com/pod-product-compliance
Lightning Source LLC
La Vergne TN
LVHW091239150826
845673LV00003B/1214